Stranger Bridgerland

John E. Olsen

Copyright © 2018 John Olsen

All rights reserved.

ISBN:
ISBN-13: 978-1974336951

DEDICATION

This book is dedicated to three people: My wonderful wife, who has always believed in me, and my loving parents who taught me hard work is a gift that keeps on giving.

CONTENTS

	Acknowledgments	i
1	MY STORY	1
2	THE GHOST AND MY DAD	8
3	GOLDEN SPIKE GHOSTS	10
4	LEFT-HAND LIGHT	14
5	LA PLATA	17
6	ENCOUNTER ON ROCK CREEK	20
7	THE TRAPPER	22
8	CHEWED OUT BY A GHOST	25
9	THE SCREAM AT MARIE SPRINGS	29
10	BIGFOOT AT THE BEAVER	32
11	BIGFOOT UP LEFT HAND	36
12	CHILDS PLAY IN LEFT HAND	42
13	THE SCOUT AT THE TABERNACLE	45
14	LITTLE GIRL AT THE CEMETERY	49
15	BLACK EYED AT THE MOVIES	51
16	I SERVED A TIME TRAVELER	55
17	UFO OVER DRY LAKE	59
18	OLD JUNIPER SHADOW	62

ACKNOWLEDGMENTS

I'd like to Thank Annie Olsen, Kim Walker, and Cody Olsen for their help in editing this book. Kate Walker for the illustrations and Hayden Snider for directing the short video promoting the launch of this book.

Also to all those who have shared their stories…

My childhood home 1960

MY STORY

I thought of which stories to include of my own for this book. I have many stories since I spent twenty years of my life living in a 100-year-old house that is haunted. Aside from the usual "Stair Monster" and voices waking me up at night, I have chosen a few stories I thought were a bit more exciting. I have never felt truly frightened in my childhood home. I have come to understand that the Stair Monster, as I call him (or them-I believe there is more than one), is very mischievous but not in any way malevolent. But to someone who didn't grow up in this house, I can see how it would be very frightening.

Bassa's Adventure

About 4 years ago, my parents asked if I would house sit while they went on a cruise. I agreed to spend a few days there to watch the house and their little dog, Bassa. Bassa is my mother's 5-year-old fat Shih Tzu.

It was Friday night and my youngest son, and I had stayed up watching TV until about 11 pm. After he fell asleep, I carried my son upstairs and came back to get Bassa. He has always slept with my parents, and when they are gone, he usually sleeps with whoever is watching the house. Bassa was asleep in his bed in the kitchen, and I decided to leave him there. I shut off all the lights, locked all the door, and went upstairs to bed.

I was awoken at 2:30 am to a horrible ruckus. I could hear banging, and Bassa was barking up a storm. I shot out of bed and headed downstairs. As I hit the landing at the bottom of the stairs, just before you can turn and see into the kitchen, the banging stopped. I stumbled in the dark to the kitchen and turned on the lights. Every cabinet door in the kitchen was open. I knew immediately that the ruckus was from the cabinet doors being opened and slammed shut repeatedly. Bassa was under the kitchen table visibly shaken.

I walked around and checked the house and doors, even though I knew it was the Stair Monster that had been in the kitchen. After checking that everything in the house was normal, I shut all the cabinet doors and scooped up Bassa from under the table. He was still shaking uncontrollably. I shut off the light and headed upstairs to bed.

I checked on my son, who was still sound asleep and Bassa climbed under the covers. As I fell asleep, he was still shivering just a bit.

It is evident that when my parents go away, the Stair Monster is most active.

"Cody?"

One afternoon when my parents were gone on a trip, my son, Cody, I and three of his friends headed to Hyrum to go fishing in our boat. After a fun day out on the water, I needed to check up on my parents' house and run some errands in Hyrum. At the house, Cody and his friends asked if they could hang out there while I ran my errands in town. "Sure," I said and headed off.

About an hour later, I came back to find all the boys sitting on the front lawn waiting for me to return. I asked why they weren't in the house as they were hastily jumping into the truck. This is the story they told me.

Right after I left to run errands, they grabbed some food from the kitchen (as boys will do) and sat down in the front room to watch a show. After about 30 minutes, a powerful sing-song female voice came from the kitchen saying "Cody!" The boys all sat up and looked at my son. The strange female voice called again, this time a little louder. She sounded as though she had stepped into the foyer right next to the front room. "Cody!" One of the boys looked at Cody and told him his grandma was calling him. With wide eyes, Cody explained that his grandparents were on vacation and they were alone in the house. They all stepped into the kitchen, but no one was around. The boys ran from the house and wouldn't go back in.

I walked through the house, but as I expected, it was empty.

The Baby Chair

When my children were young, my wife and I both worked, and my mother was kind enough to babysit a few days a week. It was always so helpful, and she was so sweet to do it. It was great to have the kids grow up so close to Grandma and Grandpa.

When my oldest was just a baby, my mother would babysit two days a week. She had been buying baby gear for him, so I didn't have to keep hauling all his things back and forth from my house to hers and back again. One day, I stopped by to see my mother, and she was excited to show me the swing she had gotten for my son. In the front room was an old green baby swing. She taught me how to put the baby in the bassinet and wind up the swing at the top and give the baby a gentle push. The baby would gently swing back and forth in the swing with a "swish…. click…. swish…. click."

At the time, we were the only two in the house since Grandpa was driving my brother to work. After she had shown me all the fun things she had found, we sat down in the kitchen to talk. It hadn't been more than 20 minutes when I heard a sound that stopped me in my tracks. I asked my mother if she could hear the sound as well. We both listened intently. Sure enough, we recognized it as the "swish.... click" of the baby swing. We stood up slowly and snuck into the front room. The baby swing was rocking wildly front to back. After a minute or two of watching in amazement, I whispered, "Maybe we wound it up, and it started swinging on its own." I had barely spoken when the swing suddenly stopped! But it didn't stop gently or wind down slowly. It stopped at the apex of the backswing as if invisible hands had grabbed the bassinet in mid-swing. It sat at the top of the backswing for about 10 seconds then the invisible hands lowered it slowly to the bottom. The seat gave a slight shutter as if it had been let go and all was quiet.

After a moment, I examined the swing. Even when I wound it up, it needed a good push to get it going. After a few tests, I also realized it did not like to swing without some weight in it. It needed the weight of a baby to keep it in motion. And what's more, I could not explain how it had stopped so abruptly.

The Tall Man

One day, in my 8th-grade year, I had just gotten home from school. As usual, I made myself a sandwich and sat down in front of the TV to relax. I was in the front room, just getting comfortable when something caught my eye. No one had come home that I knew of, so I thought that I was alone. But to my surprise, someone was walking into the front room. I watched an unfamiliar figure walk in silently. It was a tall man with overalls and a white shirt. He had a large flat brim hat, and I could see right through him. I could make out his clothing and his hat, but his face was obscured by the shadow of his hat.

I dropped my sandwich and stared in utter disbelief as he walked across the floor and sat in the rocking chair across from me and began rocking. I watched him for what seemed like a lifetime. After I gained my faculties, I closed my eyes tightly, hoping that when I opened them, he would be gone.

After a few moments of complete silence, I opened my eyes. The ghost was gone, but the rocking chair sat rocking ever so slightly. It was his way of saying he was still there. I picked up my sandwich and ran to the kitchen just as my mom walked in. It took me a few moments to gain my composure to tell her what I had seen. That's when she told me her story of the tall man.

At one point when I was young, the only bathroom in the house had a door to the kitchen and a door to my parents' room. One day I came home, and my dad was tarring the door to their bathroom down and started constructing a wall there. I remember asking why he was doing it, and he shrugged it off and said it's what mom wants.

As I sat with my mother in the kitchen, she told me the real reason for the wall. She would shut the door to the bathroom right before bed every night. Every few nights, she or my dad would wake up, and the door would be wide open and standing just inside the door was a tall skinny figure with a wide-brimmed flat hat. As soon as they turned on the light, he disappeared. It had become unnerving, and they thought putting up the wall would help.

She also told me that on a couple occasions when she would be making the bed or folding clothes, she thought my dad had walked in the room. She would start talking to him only to turn and find no one there.

THE GHOST AND MY DAD

My Dad's Story:

When I was young, my father would never admit to the existence of the ghost or allow us to talk about it. However, denying there was something in the house didn't stop the "Stair Monster" from playing tricks on him.

One Saturday afternoon, my brother, Dad, and I were the only ones at home. My brother and I were in the family room that was down in the basement at that time. My Dad had been waiting for a month to receive a package, and it had just been delivered. Back in the day, before the internet, if you wanted anything that wasn't at the store, it was ordered over the phone from a catalog. My Dad had ordered a new pair of hiking boots, and they had finally arrived.

He opened the package and was preparing to lace and try on the boots. Out of my nowhere, my Dad yelled at us from the kitchen while we were watching TV. He demanded we bring back his boot laces right away. We looked at each other in confusion and tried to explain that we had been in the basement for hours.

He had unpacked his boots and laces, then turned around to get scissors out of a drawer. As he turned back to the counter, his shoes remained, but the laces had vanished. After a few more minutes of looking all around the kitchen and all over the floor, he marched to the basement to demand we fess up.

Again, we explained that we hadn't left the basement. With a scowl on his face, my dad marched upstairs grumbling under his breath. Dad continued to search the kitchen, and then the house to no avail. Finally giving up, he headed outside to work in the yard. As he walked outside to the front porch, there, on our picnic table, folded neatly were his hiking boot laces.

Years later, my Dad finally agreed what we were saying might actually be true. You have to understand one thing about the Stair Monster. He doesn't like change. Change from the regular daily routine will bring him out. With that having been said, one winter, Dad was recovering from knee surgery and was only able to sleep sitting in his recliner in the front room. My dad sleeping in the front room was a change from the norm. The Stair Monster started to show his displeasure by running from the front room and jumping off the step to land with a big bang in the middle of the room. He did this in the middle of the night. My dad didn't sleep very well because he had to sleep through these loud gymnastics routines.

After a few nights of this, the Stair Monster started a new trick. Dad would be just about asleep when a loud two-finger cattle call would whistle right in his ear. This was followed by a mischievous laugh and footsteps running away. My Dad admitted this was unnerving as well as annoying. When he was finally able to return to sleeping in his bed, the activity slowed to the normal background noises.

To this day the Stair Monster will still let Dad know he's still around, usually with a sharp grab to his leg late at night when he is trying to sleep.

GOLDEN SPIKE GHOSTS

Jennifer's story:

In the early '80s, when my husband and I were first married, our favorite thing to do was pack up the car with camping gear on Fridays and head off. We loved to find new places to camp and, since neither one of us were from the area, we had a great time exploring. We had met at Utah State and had stayed in the valley after my husband Jon had graduated.

One weekend we invited our good friends Amy and Brian to go with us camping. We had heard the western desert was a fun trip so Friday after work we packed up and headed west. We passed the Golden Spike National Historic Site where, on May 10, 1869, the Union and Central Pacific Railroads joined their rails at Promontory Summit joining the country's railroads.

We spent the afternoon exploring the west desert including Kelton and Blue Creek, two ghost towns, in the west desert. We finally found a site that would work for our camp. It was just 20 yards from the old railroad tracks that lead from the west to Promontory Point and the Golden Spike.

After a nice tinfoil dinner and talking by the fire, we decided to go for a night hike. Not wanting to get lost in the desert, we decided to walk the railroad tracks so it would be easy to find our way back. We grabbed our jackets and headed west along the railroad tracks. After about 30 minutes, we stopped to listen to a pack of coyotes off in the hills to our right. Out of nowhere, their yelps cut off, and it became deathly quiet. As we stood there wondering what had stopped the coyotes, we heard a faint train whistle out in the distance. This was strange because it sounded like an old engine whistle, not a newer train horn. It was quiet at first but soon after a second whistle sounded louder and closer. We all stood puzzled when Jon asked, "What is that?!"

We turned to where he was pointing. In the direction the train whistle was coming from there was a light. It was a faint yellow light that seemed to have appeared from nowhere. We watched as it started to slightly sway back and forth as it got closer. It looked to be about 100 yards away on the track and quickly moving closer. We stood dumbfounded, just watching. As it got closer and closer, Amy suggested we get off the railroad tracks. Immediately we jumped into the sagebrush about 10 feet away. Watching as it continued swaying back and forth, we all tightened up our ranks with the boys taking a position just in front of us. I could feel everyone was frightened. It was all I could do not to turn around and run out into the desert!

Soon we could see an old oil lamp light, but there was no one holding it. I clamped down on my husband's arm. "There's no one holding the light," I whispered, but he said nothing. As it approached, I could hear people speaking, but it was not in English. I recognized it as Chinese! It was obviously the voices of two men having a conversation; however, I couldn't understand the language. We could hear the men but could see nothing but the lamp. It continued to float by as if invisible hands were holding it. The dialogue continued as the torch passed and forged ahead down the tracks. We stood still not even breathing as it made its way down about 100 yards further. Then we heard the train whistle again, but now from the direction, the lamp was headed. Suddenly the light went out, and we stood there in the dark, charged with adrenalin and scared to death.

After a few minutes, the coyotes began to sing again. The tension started to ease as we talked about what we had just witnessed. It took a lot of convincing from the group for me to stay the night. After we made our way back to camp, we settled in for the night. It was the last time any of us camped in the west desert.

LEFT-HAND LIGHT

John's Story

I grew up in Cache Valley. It was 1984, and I was in my late 20's. I had been chosen to be the assistant to the Teachers in my LDS ward (that's the 14-year-old boys in my church). Along with the calling came the charge to take these young men camping once a month, no matter the month. Still being somewhat of a young adult myself, I was a bit apprehensive of responsibility involved in taking six boys camping. I hadn't been much of a camper growing up but had done enough scouting to know I didn't like it. It was late October when I was called, and it was the very next Friday we were going on our first camping trip. The Teachers Quorum Adviser was around 20 years my senior but seemed like a nice guy. The camp that chosen was Left Hand Fork up Blacksmith Fork Canyon, just east of Hyrum. I didn't know much about the area but was looking forward to getting to know the boys. Turns out, scout groups go camping year around; I didn't know this. I thought camping was only a warm-weather activity. The low temperatures in October in the Cache Valley mountains range from cold to freezing. I was told to bring as much bedding as possible, just enough to not suffocate. I was very grateful I did.

We arrived at our camp 4 miles up Left Hand Fork. Our group set up camp, and the boys immediately started making a fire. We had dinner, a nice tinfoil dinner cooked in the hot coals, we told stories and jokes as the evening went on. It was getting late when one of the boys asked if we could do a night hike. I had never heard the term 'night hike,' but apparently, it's just a hike through the dark. I wasn't so sure about that, but the other adviser assured me that it was a favorite activity. We set off walking up Left Hand Fork a little ways past our camp. The road wasn't bad, but as we walked, we realized all the other camps were deserted (probably because it was late in the hunting season in October). We hadn't seen another person or vehicle since we left Hyrum.

Just as we rounded a bend in the road, the sky opened up to a prominent ridge that sloped up to the south (our right), and the lead scout stopped. He pointed at the hill and asked, "What is that?" We all stopped and looked. At the base of the ridge, there was a light. It looked like a gold, red orb bouncing up the hill. At this point, the other leader and a few boys that had fallen behind caught up to us. We watched as the light bobbed and weaved through the trees and brush up the hill. "Is it a flashlight?" one of the scouts asked. But we could all see it wasn't. It took about 4 min for the light to make it all the way to the top. Then it bounced around the top of the ridge and went out. Some of the scouts and I exclaimed, "wow!" at the same time. After a moment of unease and silence, I said, "We should head back." The other leader shook his head. "Wait just a minute." It was then that I noticed he didn't seem at all upset or frightened by the events. I was just about to ask him why when one of the boys yelled, "There it is again!" Sure enough, the light had reappeared at the base of the ridge bouncing and weaving through the trees again. We watched as it once again moved up the hill only to bounce at the top and disappear again.

Dumbfounded, we sat waiting for a half an hour to see it again, but it did not reappear. At that point, we headed back, the boys jabbering back and forth about the light. I asked the other leader how he had known, it would come back, and if he knew what it was. He told me he had seen it before and that his grandfather and dad had told him about it. "It's called the Left Hand Light," he said. He had seen it 3 times previous. He knew it would reappear because it always repeated at least 2 times, sometimes more. He said it appears some nights but not every night. His grandfather had told him that someone he knew had hiked up close to the light once. It was an old lantern with no one holding it, just a floating lantern that bobbed and weaved through the trees and brush. His dad had told him it was thought to be the spirit of a miner who had gotten lost in the hills and died. He hadn't said anything before the hike began, but he was really hoping the boys could see it.

We finished camp with no other incidents and headed for home. The boys always talked about the Left-Hand Light anytime we would camp. I have gone on that same hike three times since only once did I see it again. Its pattern through the trees never varies, and it always climbs at least 2 times.

Writers' notes: I have also been to this hill at night, and I too saw the Left Hand Light. It happens just as the story describes.

LA PLATA

Joshua's Story;

I have always loved ghost towns; even to this day, I will go out of my way to see these interesting sites. It's the history I love, not the ghost part. However, the first ghost town I visited was more ghost than it was a town.

It was the mid 80's, and I was living in Cache Valley. School was just letting out for the summer, and my friends and I were looking for an adventure. A friend of mine mentioned that he had heard of a ghost town called La Plata. This abandoned town is located at the southeast end of Cache County near Ant Flats, south of Hardware Ranch. My friend Tim and I got permission to go up through the LDS Church grounds above Porcupine Dam where we would hike the final distance into La Plata. I would like to point out that we had no idea that it was on private property.

We didn't waste any of summer break and went on Friday, the first day official day of summer break. We parked my truck around noon, at the top of the road on the Church grounds. We loaded our packs and started our hike into the town. The canyon we followed was beautiful, and the weather was perfect for the hike. The plan was to hike in, look around, and spend the night.

We reached La Plata at around 3 pm. There wasn't much left of the town except a few stone foundations and some log cabins that had almost completely decayed away. We looked around and set up our camp at the edge of the pine trees just west of the main street in the old town. We built a fire, cooked dinner, and talked about girls and the school year as the sunset. We stayed up until around 10 pm and then settled down in our tent for the night.

I was awoken at around 2 am with Tim shaking my shoulder. Even with the little light, there was in the tent, I could see his eyes were wide. I asked, "What's wrong?"

"Listen," he whispered. After a few seconds, my head cleared and it was then I could hear it. It was the faint sound of a piano playing. We sat in the tent and listened to the music for about 10 min, it was faint, but we could tell it was coming from the direction of the old main street. After a few minutes of coaxing, I talked Tim into going with me to investigate. He came mostly because he didn't want me to left him alone.

We exited the tent into the moonlit, star-filled night. We took our flashlights, but it was light enough that we didn't turn them on. As we slowly walked closer to the old main street, the sound got louder. We stopped about 75 yards west of the main street. Not only was the piano still playing, but we could hear voices too. We could see nothing out of the ordinary but stood there with our mouths agape, just listening. The sound was just what I imagined an old saloon would sound like. I could make out laughter, the piano, and the ruckus of men talking and yelling. You could just make out the sound of chairs sliding on a wood floor and glasses banging together. I tried to get Tim to go closer, but he refused. I got up the courage and started down to sneak a bit closer look myself. It got louder and louder the closer I got. Just as I reached the base of the foundation where the sound was coming from I tripped. Already extremely frightened, I let out a yell as I fell over the sagebrush. Just as I hit the ground, all went silent. Tim yelled out to see if I was ok, and I responded that I was okay. I strained for a good while to hear anything of the noises I had just heard, but all I could hear was a light breeze going through the sagebrush. All the sounds were gone.

We walked back to our camp and rekindled the fire. Neither one of us could go back to sleep. We listened all night, but the sounds never returned.

I have always wanted to go back and spend the night to see if I could hear the same thing, but it's on private land now, and no one is allowed there. I will never forget that haunting sound drifting across that sagebrush flat and will always wonder if it was an echo from the past or the old miners still enjoying a good 'ol Friday night, even in death.

ENCOUNTER ON ROCK CREEK

Tom's Story

I've spent my life in Cache Valley, and my passion has always been outdoors. There is always a cardinal rule when hunting, fishing, or hiking: DON'T GO ALONE. For the most part, I've followed that rule. It's a good rule because if you fall or get hurt or encounter any life-threatening situations, you have a friend to help or get assistance. Regardless of this rule, when we're young, we truly believe we are invincible. I was no exception.

One day, in my 20's, I got off from work early in the morning, and I had most of the day free. It was late spring, and the tributaries of the rivers were clear, a little high and perfect for fishing. I knew everyone was busy at school or work, so instead of following the cardinal rule, I loaded up my car and headed up Blacksmith Fork Canyon alone. I parked where Rock Creek met the Blacksmith Fork River, about ¾ of a mile from Hardware Ranch and headed north to fish. It was a beautiful spring day. The hills were lush and green, and there wasn't another soul for miles and miles…just me.

I fished while working my way up the canyon. I was mostly crawling through thick brush as I walked about half a mile. I got to an opening and began fishing again when all of a sudden, I had a feeling of pure terror wash over me. It was a creepy sensation as if someone had poured cold water down my back. All the hair on my neck stood up. I stopped fishing and looked around. I couldn't see or hear anything. Suddenly, it hit me that there was no noise around me. The birds and insects that had been singing up until now were dead silent. Even the river seemed muted, and I felt a crippling weight in my chest. The fear I was experiencing could only be described as overwhelmingly primal fear.

I hooked the lure onto my pole and began a short trek towards the top of the first stretch in the small canyon. There was an opening not far from me. The overwhelming feeling of apprehension and dread followed me as continued briskly toward the open hillside. I began running before I reached the clearing, and as I headed up the hill, the feeling slowly subsided. Stopping to rest and catch my breath, I quickly realized I was drenched in sweat. My pounding heart began to slow as my mind started to calm down. I sat on the hillside, examining the river and brush but could not see anything out of the ordinary. The fear had left, but I knew that I did not want to go back that same way. I hiked over the hill and made my way safely back to the truck.

In my life, I've been near bears, mountain lions, and other large animals, all of whom could do me harm. I have never felt anything like what I felt in that canyon. To this day, I do not know what was in the brush near me. But I do know it wanted to do me harm.

THE TRAPPER

Tim's Story

I grew up in Hyrum, Utah, in the early '80s. I had never given much thought to ghosts, or the paranormal other than the odd Halloween story and ghost stories around the campfire. I was raised LDS, and as a young man, I was big into scouts. I remember all my scout camps were throughout northern Utah. Summer camps at Bear Lake, fall camps in Logan Canyon. Our ward camp out at the end of summer was held in Blacksmith Fork. Camping was by far my favorite part of scouts.

My favorite scout camp was winter camp at the Quonset Huts at Camp Wapiti. Wapiti was up Blacksmith Fork about 13 miles from Hyrum. I looked forward to this camp all year. It was a Friday night filled with night games, sledding, and candy poker (my favorite). At around 9 pm, the leaders would be huddled around the stoves or in bed. We would take our bags of candy and go to the only hut with a big table, and we'd eat candy and play poker. We would bet handfuls of Jolly Ranchers, bags of M&Ms and sometimes Smarties. This trip at the end of January of '89 was no different. We got to camp and argued over who would sleep where. The top bunks were too hot; the bottom bunks were too cold, so we all fought over the middle.

We had cooked our horrible dinner (burnt Dinty Moor beef stew) around 10 pm after sledding the hill. Then we wandered back to play candy poker and warm up. There were eight scouts in my group, including my best friend, Travis. We did everything together. We all took off our snow gear, hunkered down to play a few games. Before we knew it, midnight rolled around, and we were on a massive sugar high. We debated what we should do next when someone suggested a game of hide and seek in the snow.

We immediately broke out the door into the night. The full moon had risen from behind the clouds, the mountains glowed in the moonlight, and its reflection on the snow was so bright that it seemed we could see forever. We chose someone to be the hunter, and the rest of us broke out to find a hiding spot. I decided to cross the bridge over the river and headed for a stand of small trees that lined the river. As I got to the brush, I crouched down on all fours and started to crawl along the brush, listening for the sound of anyone who might have been looking for me. The ground was covered with an icy crust that was about two inches thick. There were two to three feet of soft snow underneath. As I inched forward, the top crust of the snow would cave in, and I would have to crawl back on top.

After I crawled about 15 feet, I broke through the brush line to a clearing and stopped dead in my tracks. Across the river from me was a man standing and looking right at me. It was not someone I had ever met or anyone I expected to run into out in the woods. He looked like an old-time trapper, a young man in his late 20's but his face had seen hard times. He was in full buckskins from head to toe and wore a necklace with what looked like bear claws hanging from it. He did not have a full beard but scruff from a month or so of not shaving. In one hand, he held an old black powder rifle with leather fringe on the stalk. I could see a bone-handled knife sticking up from his belt. Below his old hat was deep gray eyes that stared at me with concern.

It felt like forever, as my brain was trying desperately to process it all, he raised his hand and motioned me to back up. I just stared in disbelief. Again, he motioned me to go back. I slowly started to back up towards the brush, trying to keep him in sight. Suddenly my foot hung up on a branch, and I looked back to free it. I quickly swung my head back around, and he was gone. I sat quietly and listened for the sound of footsteps on the hard snow, but all I could hear was the bubbling of the river. After I back out of the brush, I sprung up and sprinted to my Quonset. I undressed, jumped onto my bunk, and sat up all night thinking about what I had just witnessed.

The next morning I told no one except for my friend, Travis. He looked at me funny but could tell I was shaken. After breakfast and before we had to break camp, Travis and I walked the river on the side I had seen the Trapper. When we got to where he was standing, there were no tracks. I couldn't believe it! I looked across the river to where I had been, and my heart dropped. Right, where I had stopped, and the trapper had motioned me to go back, I saw my tracks in the snow. They had ended just before the edge of a vast cornice that overhung a deep hole swirling in the river. Had I gone any farther, I would have fallen in. With my heavy clothes and snow boots on, I would have certainly drowned. I've no idea who this ghost was or why he saved me, but I know what I saw that night, and will remember for the rest of my life. I will be forever grateful to the Ghost Trapper that saved my life.

CHEWED OUT BY A GHOST

David's Story

In the summer of 1987, I was 13 and living in Hyrum. As it often happened, I was spending the night at my best friend Brian's house. Often times, when we had a sleepover, we would sneak out to do normal kid things.

We would toilet paper someone's home or go to the Hyrum Dam to catch the skinny dippers.

On this night, I had talked Brian into going with me to TP the house of a girl I had a crush on. It was a way for adolescent boys to show their feelings without telling the girl their feelings. We had hidden the toilet paper in Brian's bedroom and had gone to bed with an alarm clock set for 2 am in case we fell asleep.

We watched movies until around 1 A.M and decided to go. With our pillowcases filled with toilet paper, we snuck out the back door and headed off to the girl's house, about 7 blocks away. When we got there, we quickly went to work. Before long, the front yard was covered in toilet paper, and we ran off towards Brian's home.

At this time of night, Hyrum was a tranquil place. At three am you wouldn't ever see cars on the streets as long as you avoided Main Street. We quickly walked home, talking, and laughing. We felt no need to be quiet because everyone was sound asleep.

As we hit Brian's street, we crossed over to the opposite sidewalk and headed to his house. Next door to Brian's house was an old brick home that had been abandoned for as long as I could remember. One time we had snuck in the back door of the home to explore. Everything was still there as though someone lived there, but everything was coated with a thick layer of dust. We hadn't stayed long because the house had a creepy vibe, and we knew we would be in big trouble if anyone found us.

As we walked the sidewalk, joking and laughing in front of the empty house, something caught my attention. I turned to look at the home, and my blood ran straight to ice. A woman was standing in the big window in the front of the house. It almost looked like she was being illuminated from the front so I could see her clearly from the waist up. She had on an old-style black dress with long sleeves that came to her wrists, there was white lace coming out from under the sleeves. The neckline on her dress came right up to her chin, and she had a large white brooch just under her neck. Her hair was in a high bun, and I remember thinking she looked like an old Librarian. She stood there with a stern, almost angry look on her face with her arms crossed in front of her. As I stopped dead in my tracks to have a better look at her, she unfolded her arms and shook a boney finger at me as if she was scolding me, but her mouth never moved.

I stood staring in fright, and couldn't move for what seemed like forever. Brian stopped and noticed I wasn't with him. He called out to see if I was okay. At the sound of his voice, I regained the use of my legs, and I bolted. I ran right past Brian and kept on going. I ran past Brian's house and all the way to my own home six blocks away. Frantically I ran through my back door and up to my room. I turned on the light and sat shaking in my bed. My dad yelled from downstairs to check on me, and I said I just come home to sleep. He muttered something and went back to bed.

It took me a week before I could tell Brian what I saw, and even when I did, he refused to believe me. I didn't walk past that house again for years. Brian tried to get me to sneak into the abandoned house again, but I wouldn't even think of it. The ghost seemed to know Brian and I had been up to no good, and she was upset with us.

Recently the house has been remodeled, and a family lives there. I sometimes wonder if the new occupants have ever seen her. I'd venture to ask, but honestly, how do you start that conversation.

THE SCREAM AT MARIE SPRINGS

Cory's Story

My father, my uncle, and I had been elk hunting for a week with no success. We had decided to try Marie Springs. It lies between Blacksmith Fork and Logan Canyon just southwest of Old Ephraim's grave.

It was late in the day, and we had decided to make one last push. We sat on a ridge overlooking a hillside with a few groves of Aspen trees. My uncle, who was getting older, needed a rest said he would sit and watch as my father and I continued on. My father and I headed down the hill. We had just made it to the bottom of the ravine when we saw my uncle frantically waving us back. Confused, we worked our way back up the hill towards him.

As soon as we reached him, my uncle asked us if we had heard that horrible sound? We told him we had not heard anything out of the ordinary. My uncle had worked with heavy equipment all his life and grown very hard of hearing. So, my dad and I were confused when he said that he had heard anything that we hadn't. My dad asked him to explain it, but he had a hard time. He said it was a loud screaming sound. But he struggled to describe it. He said it was coming from the hill that we were headed towards.

After a few minutes, my dad and uncle decided they would walk the hill. This time I was to sit and watch. I agreed, and they started back down the mountain. All was quiet as they made their way down to the ravine between the hill and where I was sitting. Just as they emerged on the hill and started across, I heard the sound. Every hair on my neck stood on end. It was a deep, loud ear-shattering screech as if a large animal was being tortured. I was 16 at the time and had spent a lot of time in the mountains. In my short lifetime, I've heard and seen and heard many things in the wild. Mountain lions, bears, injured animals but never before or ever since have I heard anything like this. It sent a wave of complete fear straight through me.

The sound seemed to be coming from a patch of dense brush in the middle of the Aspens on the hill directly across from me. As my dad and uncle worked their way across the hill and towards the target area, I desperately scanned the brush with my binoculars. I searched and searched but couldn't find anything. As my dad and uncle entered the patch where this horrible sound was coming, from it stopped abruptly. After that loud noise, the silence that filled the air was almost tangible. It was at this point I could hear my heart pounding in my ears, I was breathing heavily.

I watched intently as the two men made their way through the patch. First, my dad emerged, then my uncle. Just as my uncle walked out, there was a final loud scream from the brush. This time, it was an angry, defiant, heart-piercing scream. Then it all fell silent again; not a sound could be heard. I found a rock where I could sit and watch while trying to catch my breath.

After about 45 minutes, my uncle and dad arrived back

up the hill where I was sitting. I asked them what they had heard, and to my utter disbelief, they had not heard a sound. I explained what I'd heard, and my uncle said it had to have been what he heard earlier. Somehow, whoever was hiking near the Aspens couldn't hear or see anything out of the ordinary. We sat on the hill until dusk. All the usual forest sounds slowly returned with no sign of anything out of the ordinary. As it started to get dark, we hiked back to the truck. To this day, I can still hear the scream, but I have no idea who or what could have made such a horrible sound.

BIGFOOT AT THE BEAVER

Jon's Story

It was the mid-2000's, and I was working as a manager at the Beaver Creek Lodge up Logan Canyon. I worked 3 days on and 4 days off. Managers generally stayed at the lodge for the duration of their shift, so they didn't have to drive back and forth. It was great to not have to commute and to have 4 days off in between shifts.

I was working one night in late summer/early fall. It tended to be a little slower during this time of year. The summer travelers were all gone, but the fall rush had not started. There is not a lot to do until the trees begin to turn colors. Once fall was in full swing, we would get tourists coming up to enjoy the beauty of the canyon.

It was a Thursday night, and we only had 2 guests staying with us: a husband and wife. The couple checked in at 5 pm, and soon after, the remainder of the staff went home. I finished up my paperwork and various other duties and went to my room around 8 pm. I had fallen asleep with the TV on, and abruptly to a pounding on my door around 1:00 am. I hadn't undressed, so I got up quickly and groggily opened the door.

The husband was standing in the hallway, looking slightly nervous. He asked if they could check out immediately. Confused, I wondered if something was wrong. He hesitated for a moment then stated he and his wife were on the balcony enjoying the moonlit night when something ran across the parking lot right in front of them. I told him there wasn't anything to be afraid of. I explained that there are a lot of animals in the woods during this time of year when we didn't have many guests. Many people that visit are not used to the woods. I suspected that maybe a bear or mountain lion had scared them. He looked at me and said it wasn't an animal they had ever seen before. I asked him to describe the animal to me. He shuffled his feet and said, "It ran on two feet."

He continued to insist that he and his wife wanted to

leave. So, the two of us headed to the front desk, and I quickly checked them out. I watched as the pair threw all of their belongings in the car and sped off into the night. Shaking my head, I walked into the office to place their paperwork on the desk. I sat for a moment, gathering my thoughts. Suddenly, I had an eerie feeling I was being watched. I reached over and turned off the light on the desk. On the wall in front of me, a shadow was cast from the moonlit window onto the front of the office. It was the towering silhouette of a head on a large set of shoulders with no neck to speak of. I turned to look, but the window was so high I couldn't see what was there without standing on something to look and I wasn't interested in doing that. Fear gripped me as I slid out of the office door and stood in the hallway. Just then something slammed into the back of the building with such force I felt the blow in my guts. I quickly ran to my room, I slammed the door and sat there in shock.

I stood quietly for what seemed like an eternity when I saw lights coming down the long driveway that leads to the highway. I ran downstairs to greet a concerned highway patrolman at the front door. I brought him in, and before I could tell him what happened, he asked if I had seen anything strange. He scratched his chin as I told him what just had happened. He explained that they had received four calls about someone running across the road above the lodge in a dark suit. We both agreed that it would be a very odd thing for someone to be out here, causing trouble on a Thursday night in September.

At this point, the officer walked outside and situated himself where the shadow stood outside the window of my office. I shut off the light to see how his shadow compared to my visitor earlier. The officer was about 6'2", and whoever had been there previously had to have been at least 2 feet taller. He came back in, and we chatted for a bit. I asked him if anything else strange had happened to him in the canyon. He stated that they were not allowed to talk about the strange things that go on in Logan Canyon. He did say it wasn't his first-night chasing shadows in the area.

After he left, I sat up watching TV. I jumped at every sound. It had taken me quite a while to feel comfortable being alone at the Lodge. I was told by someone who worked there before me, that on the nights that you don't hear the coyotes, you would know that "they" are around. Coyotes don't like sasquatches.

BIGFOOT UP LEFT HAND

Sean's Story

In 1992, when I was 21, some college friends and I thought we'd go camping for the long Memorial Day weekend. One of my buddies was a city kid from Washington, other was a full-blood Navaho from the reservation. They were both graduating from Utah State, and we wanted to have one last hoorah before we all parted ways. They'd just finished finals, and we were all leaving by next Wednesday.

It was a busy camping weekend, and we didn't want to be around a lot of people. So, we eliminated Logan Canyon because we didn't want to be in a crowded campground. I was familiar with the Left Hand Fork up Blacksmith Fork Canyon and thought if we could make it up to the end of the canyon, we probably wouldn't see many people.

On Friday afternoon, we left USU and headed to our campsite. We weren't in a hurry, and when we arrived no one was there, so we set up camp. We camped at the end of the vehicle access road. The only campers we passed on the way in were three-quarters of a mile to the west of us, and they were an older couple. We saw them on our way up the canyon as we stopped to look for fish in the creek. The road was pretty rough, even for a well modified off-road vehicle. It was a pretty nasty road from our camping site eastward up to Hardware Ranch.

There was a beaver pond right next to the campsite last time I had been up there, but it was mostly gone. I think the state came in and trapped all the beavers to improve the fishing. At about 4:00 PM, I started fishing on the flat sandy part around the remains of the beaver pond. As I fished, my buddies set up camp.

Later, we had our dinner and just sat around talking. We lit a fire when it got dark, nothing seemed out of the ordinary. At 10:30 pm, we were surprised to hear a big splash in the beaver pond. My city friend had never been out in the woods much, was very uneasy. He stood up and freaked out, staring in the dark to see what might have made the noise. I told him to relax, it was probably just a beaver slapping its tail on the water. I was familiar with that noise from other times I'd camped in the woods.

Two minutes later came the same noise, another splash. The second time it happened I was purposely paying attention, we had a break in the conversation. This time I had gotten a good sense of the splash. It sounded a little odd, like a 'ka-thump,' and sounded like a big rock being thrown into the river. I blew it off as just another beaver. It was shortly followed by two more splashes and this time they sounded like even larger rocks being thrown into the water. We thought the beaver was pretty agitated and must not like us being there. Again, I blew it off.

Ten minutes later, I heard another sound, a thumping noise. It sounded like a thump being generated by something significant hitting the ground. I realized the sounds were coming from the area where I had been fishing earlier that afternoon. Grabbing a flashlight, I slowly walked to the beaver pond. To my complete surprise, I saw five or six large uneven rocks, each about the size of a bowling ball. I started inspecting the stones. I didn't remember them being there in the afternoon. I also saw that the stones were lying on top of the large wader boot prints I had left in the sand and mud. "Gosh," I thought. When I realized the rocks weren't there that afternoon, I began trying to figure out just how they would have gotten there. I walked back up to the campfire, about 30 feet away and asked if my friends had moved the rocks there. They denied it, and I believed them because we'd been together all afternoon, except when I was fishing. I was the only one who had walked down by the lake. I wasn't crazy…

While we were discussing the rocks, trying to figure out where they came from, we heard something trying to walk softly through the aspen grove across the stream. A hushed low growl was barely audible. We blew this off too, rationalizing it as a deer or an elk. My buddy freaked out again, and this time, it took a few minutes to calm him down again. We heard the soft grunting again, but this time the volume of the growl increased and changed to a loud raspy scream! From that moment on, the volume increased exponentially, and the sound reverberated across the sides of the canyon.

The noise was ten seconds in length, and I could feel it in my chest. The scream elevated to sound that I can only compare to nails being dragged across a chalkboard or like a woman screaming for her life. The growl/scream had the intensity of a bull horn pointed right at us. I could feel my shirt collar vibrating. I don't think it was the wind, but the loud vocalization that reverberated through me. After the scream, something large ran through the mountainside, breaking large branches in its path. From my estimation, it traveled about 100 ft. My skittish friend from Washington was now inconsolable. I was freaking out too, and couldn't rationalize the noise anymore. I honestly didn't know what it was. I have heard mountain cats, bears, elk, and an occasional moose but this was unlike anything I've ever heard. It was an unexplainable sound. It echoed off the whole canyon, off the walls, off the cliffs to the north of us, and back down through the canyon.

This put us all on edge. However, after it had charged that short way up the mountain, things settled down. However, there were no bug sounds or other normal outdoors sounds, nothing. The only sound was the stream and crackle of our campfire. We were all jumpy and paranoid. Nothing happened the rest of the night. Questions started playing through my mind….was it elk….cougar…. maybe a hoax? We had nothing with us to defend ourselves other than a baseball bat. We all had a strong impression that whatever made the noise did not want us there. Somehow, I knew this wasn't a person, it was something more significant. But whatever it was, it showed aggressive behavior directed towards us!

We stayed awake until about 2:00 am and didn't hear anything new. We finally fell asleep.

The next morning, I woke up a little before 5:00 am to catch some trout for breakfast. As I exited my tent, I was still pondering what had happened the night before. I looked up the mountain where we'd heard all the crashing. Just above me, probably 100 yards away, still back-lit by the sky, was a small aspen and juniper grove by a cliff. I saw a sizeable upright figure. I saw mostly a character, but it was walking upright. It reached out with its right arm and kind of pushed couple of aspen trees. I got a good view of the side of its arm, and it was rather large. I observed it for about 8-10 seconds, then it quickly disappeared behind a rock pillar.

My buddies were still in the tent, and I was in shock, trying to figure out what this was. I knew for sure I'd seen an arm and observed it walking on two feet. It was too massive to be human. I was trying to attach the silhouette to any animals I might know of, and I couldn't do it. Was that a moose walking away somehow? Did his antler bump the tree? I had a hard time wrapping my head around it. That was pretty much the end of it. I was concerned after last nights' vocalization that whatever it was might come across the creek, but I wasn't concerned enough to pack up and rush home to contact the sheriff's department. I have seen a cougar before while grouse hunting. But, last night's events, with the loud scream, was much more frightening than the cougar.

My buddies got up at about 9:00 am. My Navajo friend and I got into a discussion about creatures in the legends of the Navajo Nation. Neither of us could really explain what it was, a legend or not. If you had asked me the prior week if I believed in Bigfoot, I would have said no. Previously, the only idea of Sasquatch I had ever had was from some books in elementary school. I knew about the Patterson-Gimlin film, but in my mind, Bigfoot only existed in Oregon, Washington and California. I had also heard stories about Boy Scout sightings in the mid-70's.

In the years after our encounter, once I moved up to Oregon, I would hear a story here or there about Sasquatch and instead of dismissing it, would start reading. I started learning more about what society knows about Bigfoot. It has taken me fifteen years to realize this encounter was most likely a Sasquatch. Back when this happened, my friends and I knew nothing about the rock throwing, typical vocalization, etc... It took me all these years and a fair amount of studying, to piece together what really happened.

CHILDS PLAY IN LEFT HAND

Colton's Story

My son and I love the outdoors. If we aren't fishing or hunting, we are hiking or rock hounding. On most days, we can be found outdoors. It's a passion we have always shared. One late spring Saturday, around mid-May 2007, my 8-year-old son and I decided to enjoy some time in the mountains. This time of year, the back roads in the Cache National Forest are finally opening up for travel. My son and I had gotten our list of honey-do's and chores done by noon. It was a beautiful Saturday, so we packed the truck with our fishing poles, rock hammers, and binoculars and headed up Blacksmith Fork Canyon.

We settled on driving up Left Hand Fork as far as we could, and spent the rest of the afternoon fishing, hiking, hunting for deer sheds, and looking for fossils in the shale. We enjoyed one of the best days just being in the outdoors.

As the sun dipped behind the mountains, we loaded up and headed home. As we traveled down the road, we talked about the day. We talked about when we wanted to come back, and everything we wanted to do. After driving only about a mile down the road, out of nowhere, the truck gave a big jerk and BANG! I heard the distinctive sound of metal and plastic crumpling and felt a shudder in the steering wheel. I slammed on the brakes, and we came to a complete stop. I have been driving long enough to know that we'd had a collision and I knew I had hit something big. We had only been going 15-20 mph, but the impact had caused our seat belts to lock up on us. I checked on my son to make sure he was ok. We were both rattled but unharmed. I told him we must have hit a boulder or rock that had slid down the hill and I needed to check the truck. I could not remember seeing anything in the road before the impact but knew from the sounds and feel that there was real damage waiting for me at the front of my truck.

I got out and walked to the front of the vehicle. In my mind, I was already calculating how far up the canyon we were and how we would have to walk out if the truck wasn't drivable. I was worried because we had not seen another soul all day and knew we would have to walk to the main canyon to get a signal on my cell phone.

As I walked around to the front, I was in complete shock. There was no damage at all to the front of the truck. I ran my hands over the bumper and looked all around but didn't see anything. I was so confused. I got down and looked underneath, but everything was in perfect condition. I signaled my son to pop the hood. I searched the engine over but could find nothing wrong. I shut the hood and walked around the truck to find nothing out of place. There were no rocks, no wood, absolutely nothing that should have caused the truck to act like it had. The engine was in perfect working condition, and there was no damage anywhere.

Dumbfounded, I stood there, trying to figure out what might have happened to have felt like we were in an unfortunate accident. As I stood there in the fading light, I was about to get back in the truck when I heard something in the brush to my right, just on the other side of the stream. It was children laughing. It sounded like 2 or 3 young kids laughing at me. The hair on my neck shot up as I strained to see what, or who was across the stream. The laughing continued as I nervously scanned brush to see who was making the noise. The evening was dead still, with no wind, and I could see nothing in the bush or trees. I was about to bolt for the door on my truck when all of a sudden more laughter ensued. It was more children's laughter, but now it was also coming from the left in the trees on the hill above me. I froze, wondering what was going on. I knew there were no kids up there, and my mind raced with what else it could be. I yelled out to see who was there, but I was only met with more laughing. I stood there, trying to make out exactly what was going on when I realized the laughter seemed to be getting closer. I snapped to my senses and quickly jumped in the truck and put it in gear. We sped off without any problems like nothing had happened to the truck. I sped down the dirt road as fast as I dared go.

My son asked me what was wrong; I simply told him everything was ok, and we must have just hit a big pothole. He had not heard any of the sounds, and I didn't want to frighten him. It took quite a while before I ventured up Left Hand again. This was the one and only time I've experienced anything like this and I hope it was the last.

THE SCOUT AT THE TABERNACLE

Kevin's Story

It was in the early '90s, my wife, Tiffany, and I had just gotten married. We lived in an apartment in Logan while I was going to school at USU. We both worked the graveyard shift. This was great because we could just keep our schedule of staying up at night and sleeping during the day on weekends as well. Our favorite thing to do when we weren't working was to go on night walks through Logan. Our usual routine took us down 5th north to 2nd East then over past the Temple down 2nd north to turn and walk south behind the Logan Tabernacle. Then we would head down to 3rd south up to the main street and back home. It was so beautiful and peaceful at night.

One night in the middle of the week, Tiffany and I happened to both have the night off. We had finished our shopping at Smith's grocery store and had unloaded everything at home. It was about 3 am, and we decided to do our nightly walk. Everything was beautiful. The moon was nearly half full, there was the occasional car passing or a barking dog, but for the most part, 3 am in Logan is very still. We had passed the temple and turned down 2nd headed toward the Tabernacle. It was at this point I caught the distinct smell of campfire in the air. It was the middle of July; though not unusual to smell a fire, this was a powerful smell. I looked at Tiffany, and she agreed she could smell it too. We reached the corner of 2nd North and 1st east and crossed to the sidewalk that ran past the back of the Tabernacle. Up until this point, I hadn't seen anything out of the ordinary.

As we approached the tabernacle and turned to pass the pine trees on the northeast corner, a flickering light caught my attention. We slowed our pace and turned to see a campfire just to the left of one of the trees and sitting on a log stump next to the fire was a boy. He looked to be about 12-14 years old and had a wide-brimmed scout hat and an old scout uniform on. Having been a scout and seen old pictures and paintings of scouts, I knew what the older uniforms looked like. He was looking in the fire and poking at it with a stick. I found it extremely odd that someone would let him build a fire on the Tabernacle lot or to camp there at all. As our walk brought us closer to him, we stopped to get a good look. Just then he looked up with a snap of his head. He looked startled to see us, and he had a confused, frightened look on this face. I didn't want to alarm him, so I smiled and nodded my head, my wife did a little wave, and we started walking again. He did a slight wave of his own, and with big eyes, he watched us walk away.

As we walked on, my wife and I wondered what a scout would be doing camping at the Tabernacle. I explained to Tiffany how strange it was that the uniform seemed old, but still looked brand new. By the time we reached the south corner of the tabernacle, I had convinced Tiffany we had to go back and make sure he was ok. We hadn't seen anyone else, and if it was a prank, it needed to be dealt with.

We turned and headed back to the trees. As we got closer, I noticed the smell of campfire that was so thick before was now gone. As we arrived at the spot where we should have been able to see the fire, we saw nothing. We closed in on the area and were greeted by darkness. He was gone. I let go of Tiffany's hand and walked over to the trees and found no sign of a fire. No fire pit, no logs, nothing. Not even a hint of smoke in the air. Completely puzzled, I called my wife over to investigate. We could not believe what we were witnessing, or should I say NOT witnessing. We compared notes as to what we had seen, and we both agreed on what we had observed.

After checking to see if we had missed anything in our exploration, we hurried off for home. For weeks after, we walked the same path, hoping to see the young boy again but every night we were disappointed. We kept this experience between my wife and me, but we often talked about what it might have been. Was it a ghost, a shared hallucination, or someone playing an elaborate prank? Nothing seemed to add up. Then one day, many years later, I was at the dentist office waiting for my checkup. On the table was a book with old photos of Cache Valley. I picked it up and started flipping through the pictures. I stopped on a page and almost dropped the album. There, in black and white, was a picture of scouts camping around a fire on the northeast corner lawn of the Tabernacle in the early 1900s. I sat and studied the picture. I didn't recognize "our" scout, but it was definitely the same period and same uniforms as the scout was wearing that night.

After mulling this over, I formulated a theory in my mind. After thinking it over and talking to my wife, we believe we had a moment when we could see through a window in time. How the scout had reacted to our presence revealed he was as shocked to see us as we were to see him. I often wonder if he told anyone of the night he saw two strange people in odd clothes walking past his camp that night at the Logan Tabernacle.

LITTLE GIRL AT THE CEMETERY

Tina's Story

I was babysitting my 3-year-old grandson for the day. My son had dropped him off, and we had gone through our regular routine for the day. It was time for him to watch TV and have a nap on the couch. We had just eaten lunch and were ready to settle down when the power went out. With no electricity, there was no TV. We tried reading a book, but my grandson was having none of it.

I decided maybe he would fall asleep on a car ride, so I loaded him up in his car seat and headed out on a drive. As I drove around Hyrum, my grandson chattered away, asking me all kinds of questions. I decided to take a slow ride through the cemetery. As we leisurely made our way around, I stopped at my niece's grave to see if any old flowers needed to be taken off. I sat looking over the gravestones when I heard my grandson start talking in the back of the car. "No! NO!" he demanded. I looked in the rear-view mirror to see if he was ok. He sat with a deep scowl on his face and his arms folded. He was looking out the window which I had rolled down so he could get some air. "NO! I don't want to play!" he said and turned his head away from the window.

"Cody, what's wrong?" I asked him. He looked at me with a scowl on his face. "I don't want to play," he demanded. "Play?" I questioned. "Play with who?"

"That little girl in the white dress!" he said and pointed out the window. I looked around to see if anyone was there, but I could see no one. "Cody, no one is there," I said. He looked indignantly at me and pointed again. "That little girl in the white dress Grandma, she is asking me to go play, and I don't want to!" I looked out the window hoping to see what he was talking about, but I could see no little girl. Then suddenly, something caught my eye. There, right where Cody was pointing, was a small old gravestone. As I looked, I realized it was the grave of a young girl. Suddenly my blood ran ice cold.

"I told you, no!" Cody yelled out the window. At that moment, I was done. I quickly put the car in gear, and we sped off towards home. After taking Cody out of the car, I asked him to describe the girl to me. He would just say she had a white dress and a cut on her neck. He kept saying he didn't want to go with her. I comforted him and told him it was ok.

When we got home, the power had returned, and we sat down to watch some tv. After a few moments, my grandson was all but asleep. As I walked out of the room, he looked at me with droopy eyes and said, "If that girl comes here, Grandma, don't let her in. She scares me." And he fell asleep. A slight shudder ran through me. I often wonder what younger kids see that we cannot. I do believe the veil between worlds is thinner for them.

BLACK EYED AT THE MOVIES

Jill's Story

My strange encounter was in the early '90s when I lived in Logan. I was originally from northern California and had chosen to go to USU for school. It was the spring of my freshman year, and I lived with three other girls in an apartment just off campus. The four of us had become pretty good friends and did quite a lot together.

One night we had all decided to go to a movie, but for one reason or another, all three of my roommates had something come up and couldn't go. It was a late movie and didn't start until 9 pm. I didn't really feel like going alone but by 8:30 there was nothing on TV, and I was bored. So, I bundled up and headed to the theater.

It was the old theater by the Cache Valley Mall; the parking lot was almost empty except for all the people I assumed were watching the 7 pm showing. I had to park pretty far from the entrance. It was freezing, I pulled my coat on tight, locked my car and headed for the doors. Being only 18 and alone, I was on very high alert. I knew my mother would have had a fit if she knew I was out alone in the dark going to the movies. But in my mind, I had become familiar with Logan and felt relatively safe. I bought my ticket and a drink and headed to my seat. I had chosen to see White Fang. I had read the book many times, and I loved Ethan Hawke. There were only two other people in the theater, a couple in their 30s. I took my favorite seat about halfway back in the middle and watched the movie.

After the movie, I sat through the credits and waited for the couple to leave. I felt a little stupid being alone and didn't want to walk out with the couple. I left and threw my cup in the garbage, went to the restroom, and bundled up to walk out to my car. I knew it would be cold outside and in the car. One of the employees that were cleaning up in the concessions area thanked me for coming. I smiled and walked out. As I stepped out into the cold, I looked out across the parking lot and at the mall. My car and two others, most likely the people working at the movie theater, were the only cars in sight.

Just as I was about to head to my car, something caught my eye. Two figures were standing just outside the doors of the mall. They didn't look very tall, and my first thought was they must be just teenagers hanging out. It was so late, the mall had been closed since before I arrived at 9, and it was so cold. I worried for a minute but figured it was not my problem, and I headed for my car. I kept alert as I walked at a quick pace to my car. I couldn't see them heading my way, but I had a heavy feeling come over me. I got to my car and unlocked it, quickly swinging into my seat. It was at this point I noticed a small amount of frost had covered my windshield. I started my car and turned on the defrost.

Suddenly, I heard a loud knock on the driver side window and jumped. I looked out to see the two figures standing just outside my car door. They both had dark gray hoodies on that covered their faces down to their nose; I couldn't see their eyes at all. I realized that they were not teenagers at all, just kids. The smaller one was standing just outside of the car; she looked to be about 8 years old. The other, a boy, standing back a bit, seemed to be about 10. My mind raced; it could only have been a minute at most since I had seen them standing just outside the mall, and yet they had covered 150 yards in that short time. My head was spinning when the little girl knocked again and gave the gesture to roll down my window. Every cell in my body was screaming for me to leave RIGHT NOW, but I couldn't see out of my windshield yet. In my mind I tried to push back the dread, thinking, "They're just kids, what is there to be scared of? Maybe they need help?"

I relented and rolled the window down about 2 inches just enough so we could talk. As I did, the little girl spoke, "Sister, could my brother and I get a ride home?" The little girl's voice had a sad, pleading tone. "Where are your parents?" I asked her. "Momma was going to pick us up after the movies, but she didn't. Can we get in your car?" I felt torn! My mind kept saying they were just two kids freezing, and I needed to help, but something deep down was screaming, "NO!!" I can only describe it as primal fear, I had never felt this way before. The more I hesitated, the more determined they got. "Please, we are so cold. Maybe we can just warm up in your car?"

I sat frozen inside; I honestly didn't know what to do. I told the little girl, "There are people in the theater, and they can let you use their phone to call your mom. And it's warm in there." "NO!" she spat out at me, and I could tell it came out more harshly than she had meant. But when she said it, it shook me, and I knew at that moment I couldn't, under any circumstance, let them in my car. At this point, the boy stepped a little closer to my car and in a curt voice said, "You have to invite us in, or we can't get in your car. We are just little children. We aren't going to hurt you or anything. Just let us in." At this point, the little girl had raised her head just enough I could see most of her face, and what I saw made my blood run ice cold. She had an ashen complexion and a beautiful sweet face, but her eyes were shiny and completely black. I froze momentarily.

After a few seconds, I managed to squeak out a loud, "NO!" and I threw the car into gear and took off. I turned on the windshield wipers. Luckily the heat must have been on just long enough because it cleared off and I sped out of the parking lot. I didn't look back as I drove home. I pulled into the driveway and ran into the house. I was afraid that the kids would be right behind me when I got out, but I made it in the house. I collapsed on the floor of the entryway sobbing. All my roommates came running out of their rooms and helped me to the couch. I sobbed for nearly an hour before I calmed down enough to recount the story.

To this day, I don't go out alone at night. As I have gone over the experience in my mind, a few things have come to my attention that didn't before. The way the little girl spoke is not how a little girl speaks, at least not for these days. She called me "sister," and at the time, I was not LDS. I had many friends who were LDS, and that is what little kids at church call the ladies at church. Also, the girl said phrases like "my brother and me." That is not how kids talk. The feeling I had as they spoke to me wasn't just fear, it was a deep-seated terror that I hadn't ever felt before or experienced since.

I SERVED A TIME TRAVELER

David's Story

It was the spring of 1992, I was 17 and worked at Arby's in Logan. I had worked there for about 3 months, and I knew the routines. It was my first job outside of working on the farm as a kid.

For those who don't know Cache Valley and Logan, it has a huge LDS population. As such, in the '80s and '90s, there were not a lot of businesses open on Sundays. The

Arby's just west of the Cache Valley Mall was. The Mall was never open on Sundays, but Arby's was.

Working on Sundays was incredibly dull, but we all had to take our turn working it. I didn't mind working Sundays because it was so slow and I could just putter around. There were only two people on shift at any given time on Sunday and if you got the right person working with you, it really wasn't bad.

I've really not been big into the paranormal my whole life. However, something really very strange happened to me one Sunday afternoon.

I had just gotten home from church when I got a call from a coworker. She asked if I could take her shift that Sunday afternoon and that she would trade me by taking my Friday next week. Of course, I jumped at the chance to have a Friday evening off work.

I arrived around 2 pm, and as usual, there were no customers there. The guy I was relieving gave a quick wave and left. I went to the back where the person I was working with was sitting, reading a book. This was frowned upon, but I really didn't care myself. I spent the next hour stocking condiments and washing the last of the dishes.

It was close to 3:30 when the chime at the front door rang. My coworker didn't even look up from his book, so I headed up front. What greeted me was a man that looked like he'd walked out of an Old Norse Legend. He was a younger man in his mid to late '20s and was at least 6'7" tall. I'm 5'10," and he towered over me. He had long red hair tied in a bun in the back and a long red beard that hung to his chest. He wore authentic Viking gear, including worn leather and a large knife on his belt. What really caught my eye was the long ax slung over his back; it was authentic and looked well used, and very sharp. His arms had healed scars on them, and his face was tired and worn down. I stared while he stood there, staring at the menu.

"Can I help you?" I asked. I really couldn't think of anything else to say. He looked down at me and ordered a meal to go. He spoke English, but with an accent, I couldn't quite put my finger on. I told him his total was $5 something. He took something from his side, a worn leather pouch. He dumped it out on the counter and started to dig through the coins. I couldn't help but notice that he had all kinds of coins, most of which I've never seen before. With large callused hands, he picked up $6 worth of 1960 silver dollars and scooped the rest back in the leather pouch. I offered him his change, but he dismissively waved it off.

I went to the back and made his sandwich, keeping an eye on him. He just stood there patiently until it was done. I handed him his bag, and he nodded and headed out the door. At this point, I really wanted to see what a Viking drove, so I hurried around the counter and to the door looking everywhere…nothing. There was no vehicle, and I couldn't see him. Thinking maybe he had walked towards the mall, I stepped out the door and looked around but couldn't see anything. He could have run around the building, but in this amount of time, he couldn't have driven or walked too far away.

I wandered back in contemplating my experience. I decided to keep it to myself. I've really only told a few people for fear of someone thinking I'm nuts. I don't know who he was. In my mind, though, I really like to think I met a time traveler.

UFO OVER DRY LAKE

Delmont's Story

It was the mid 50's, and I had worked for the Utah State Road Department for about 8 years. I had been hired after I returned from World War II.

My crew and I had been assigned to work the newest portion of Sardine Canyon, just below the old work sheds on US 89. It was late spring, just before dawn. We were working on repairing winter damage and doing general maintenance.

Just before the sun broke the sky, one of the crew

members noticed something strange at the top of Babbit Shanty Hill just to the northeast of where we were working. I pulled out a pair of binoculars I had in my truck, and I scanned the object. It was silver and very reflective. It seemed to sit right on the very top of the hill not moving at all. It was hard to tell exactly how big it was from the angle we had. I passed the binoculars around, and everyone got a good look. After a while, we all had decided it was one of the military weather balloons that were made out of the gleaming foil material.

I got everyone focused again, and we started the day's work. We were within sight of the balloon all morning. At lunch, we drove up to the sheds to see if we could get a better look at what it was on the hill. I scanned it again with the binoculars but still could not see anything but a shiny silver dome sitting at the top of the mountain. I had nearly talked myself into taking a hike to see it for myself but thought better of it. It was a good hike, and we still had a lot of work to do.

It was the end of the day, and the sun had just set behind the Wellsville Mountains about half an hour ago when I decided to call it a day. As dusk was descending, we loaded our gear in the trucks and headed for the sheds. Just as we started driving, the truck in front of me slammed on its brakes, and everyone jumped out, pointing back at Babbit Shanty Hill. I looked back and saw that the silver object wasn't silver anymore. It had turned a bright orange-red color. I was thinking it was the last of the sun's rays that were lighting it up when all of a sudden it started to lift off of the hill. I got out of my truck, making sure not to take my eyes off of it. It stayed hovering over the hill for a couple minutes, and I could see lights underneath it. As we all stood outside our trucks, in shock, it started to silently drift off the hill. As it got closer and closer to us, I could make out better details of the object. I could see it was round with a flat bottom and a dome on top. There were 5 lights on the underside, 4 smaller white lights around the perimeter of the object and a much bigger red light right in the center. As it drifted closer to us, I could see the outer surface.

What had been silver was now an odd gleaming color of orange and red. The skin seemed to glow in a way I've never seen before. It appeared to me to be about 50 yards across, and it made no sound as it moved across the Dry Lake Valley. We were parked just to the south of Dry Lake, just before you hit the base of the hill. The object glided down to Dry Lake and then turned and headed straight towards the Wellsville Mountains. As it was just about to hit the base of the mountain, there was a quick flash at the bottom of the object, and it shot straight up. In an instant, it was gone. If I had blinked, I would have not seen where it had gone because it was so fast.

We all stood quietly in the road, staring up at the darkening sky. No one spoke for a long time. We loaded up and headed to the sheds. As we all parked the trucks, we collectively decided not to tell anyone what we had seen. We were all practical men and worried about what anyone would think of us. We all thought it was best to not have people think we were off our rockers. To this day, I have no idea what we saw. But, I'm thrilled I never took that hike at lunch.

OLD JUNIPER SHADOW

Tammy's Story:

In the late '80s, I was in my early 20's and going to an LDS Single Adult ward. My best friend, Jen, and I were asked on a date by two young guys in the ward for a Saturday night in early September. We happily agreed to go. The guys, Eric and Tim, told us to wear hiking clothes and to bring a jacket. Hiking was a typical date activity at the time.

Saturday evening came, and the boys picked us up at 7 pm. We went to dinner and then watched a movie at one of their houses. At around 10 pm, we headed up Logan Canyon. The boys explained we were going on a night hike. My date, Eric, explained that the moon was nearly full. Even though we had flashlights, we really wouldn't need them since the trail would be illuminated in the dark. Surprisingly, he was right. We parked the car and headed up the path on the moonlit trail.

We were laughing and having a great time as we hiked. We came to a location where the trail dipped down, and an open space with no trees was visible except for a small group to the left. We stopped to get a drink of water and talk. We sat on a few large boulders just off the trail that offered a beautiful view of the whole area.

We laughed and chatted for about 15 min when Jen

pointed out something coming across the sagebrush flat down the trail. It looked like a tall skinny figure traveling rather fast. We all stopped talking and watched as it moved down the trail. I started to get slightly uncomfortable as it got closer. Eric and Tim thought it was probably just another hiker coming down the path, but I could tell they were a little uneasy. We hadn't seen anyone parked or camping at the trailhead. After a few minutes, the figure moved close enough to know it was very tall. I could make out the shape of a head and shoulders, but I couldn't see legs. It seemed to be floating as there was no up and down motion as it moved. I suggested we leave, but no one moved; it was like we were mesmerized by it. It was so much darker than the shadows that were around it.

As the dark form got closer, my fear increased. When it reached the bottom of the little incline we were at the top of, Eric yelled, "Hello!?" As he did, it came to a stop. Eric called out to see if they were ok, but there was no reply. It was quiet, with not even a breath of wind. Suddenly, the shadow started gliding up the trail towards us again. Jen and I grabbed hands. We were both visibly shaking. Eric called out, and again it stopped. It was close enough now I could see the form was so dark that it was not just a shadow but seemed to be the complete absence of light. It was so tall but thin for its massive height.

Suddenly, Tim, who had the strongest flashlight, turned it on and pointed it at the figure. As soon as the light hit it, it vanished! He shined the light back and forth, looking for the character, but we could see nothing. I insisted we leave right then. Jen and I turned on our lights and headed down the trail. The boys were right behind us as we stumbled back to the car. I was so scared I could not bring myself to look back. We swiftly sped down the canyon, and it wasn't until we hit Logan that we all relaxed. The boys dropped us off without talking much. To this day, I haven't gone night hiking again. I have no idea what we saw that night. I have never seen anything so dark black. Like was like looking into….. nothingness.

ABOUT THE AUTHOR

John Olsen lives in Nibley, Utah in beautiful Cache Valley with his wife and 3 children. He has spent 30+ years researching and collecting paranormal stories for this book series. John is still collecting stories and would love to hear from you. You can contact him at olsenj243@gmail.com

Look for other books from Author John Olsen
Stranger Bridgerland
Beyond Stranger Bridgerland
Stranger West

Printed in Great Britain
by Amazon